ESTEVAN

WALKING ACROSS AMERICA

by

Mary Dodson Wade

COLOPHON HOUSE HOUSTON, TEXAS

For Marj,
who marches with me
across the pages of Texas history
-- M.D.W.

[The story of the Narváez expedition is found in *La Relacíon que dio Alvar Nuñez Cabeça de Vaca....*, generally known as *The Narrative*, printed in Zamora, Spain, in 1542. Estevanico's final days are recorded in *The Story of the Discovery of the Seven Cities* by Fray Marcos de Niza, published in *His Own Personal Narrative of Arizona Discovered by Fray Marcos de Niza who in 1539 First Entered These Parts on his Quest for the Seven Cities of Cibola*, translated from the original Spanish, printed in Topawa, Arizona, 1939.]

Cataloging-in-Publication Data

Wade, Mary Dodson
Estevan, Walking Across America / by Mary Dodson Wade.
 p. cm.
Summary: An account of the life of Estevanico, a dark-skinned slave from Morocco, one of four survivors of a Spanish expedition to the New World in 1527.
1. Estevan, d. 1539—Juvenile Literature. 2. Southwest, New—History—to 1848—Juvenile Literature. 3. America—Discovery and Exploration—Spanish—Juvenile Literature [1. Estevan, d. 1539. 2. Southwest, New—History. 3. American—Discovery and Exploration] I.Title
ISBN 1-882539-11-7
ISBN 1-882539-12-5(pbk)
E125.E8 1994
971.092
[B]

Published by Colophon House
10700 Richmond, #205
Houston, TX 77042-4905

$\mathcal{N}$early five hundred years ago, five ships sailed from Spain. Each ship carried more than a hundred passengers. On one was a dark-skinned slave from Morocco named Estevan. He was travelling with his master, army captain Andrés Dorantes.

Among the passengers sailing to the New World that June day were soldiers, priests, Spanish noblemen, servants, and even an Aztec prince who was returning home.

The leader, Pánfilo de Narváez, squinted into the distance with his good eye. Seven years earlier he had lost the sight in the other eye while fighting in the New World. Still, Narváez was eager to return. The king of Spain had made him governor of Florida.

No one knew how large Florida was. On the map it covered all the land near the Gulf of New Spain. But it was not the size of the place that made Narváez anxious to get there.

Other places in the New World had gold and silver, and Narváez was sure he would find some. He would have to give the king part of it, but, no matter, he would still be wealthy.

Second in command of the expedition was Alvar Nuñez Cabeza de Vaca, a man whose name meant "face of a cow." He too hoped to become wealthy.

After a peaceful voyage across the Atlantic Ocean, the ships stopped at an island to get horses. Then, a terrible hurricane sank two of the ships. Estevan and Dorantes were safe, but everyone was so afraid of the storms that they spent the winter in a safe harbor in Cuba.

When spring came, they again set sail for Florida and came ashore near a beautiful body of water we call Tampa Bay.

Narváez raised a flag and read a speech saying he was the new governor. He told the Indians that they belonged to the King of Spain. No Indians were in sight, and even if they had heard the speech, they wouldn't have understood a word.

The Spaniards were disappointed to find only one small gold object in a deserted Indian village. Narváez wanted to search for more, but the others argued with him. "We should stay with the ships," they said, but Narváez would not listen.

He ordered three hundred men and forty horses to go inland to see if they could find gold. Then he sent the ships to a harbor he thought was nearby. "We will meet you there," he said, not knowing they would never see the ships again.

Cabeza de Vaca did not agree with Narváez, but he mounted his horse. Captain Alonzo del Castillo Maldanado and Captain Dorantes rode at the head of their soldiers. Estevan stayed near his master.

The Indians were terrified of the horses and strange men in armor. They hid as the Spaniards struggled through swamps and climbed over trees knocked down by a hurricane. There was no food to eat.

Finally the soldiers captured four Indians who told them there was corn and gold at Apalachen (near Apalachicola, Florida). The Spaniards nearly starved before they found it.

At Apalachen there was food but no gold. Then the Indians attacked. The Spaniards assumed their armor would protect them, but the arrows went right through. The Aztec prince fell dead, and the Spaniards fled to the coast. When they got there, no ships were in sight.

The Spaniards were desperate. Fifty men had died, and many others were sick. "If we just had boats," they said, "we could sail to New Spain." They didn't know that New Spain (Mexico) was a thousand miles away. Besides, no one knew how to make boats.

Then one man said, "I think I can make a furnace." They built the furnace and melted their stirrups and buckles. They made tools and nails. They cut trees and nailed boards together. They made sails out of their shirts and braided ropes from horses' tails.

Finally, five boats were ready to sail. Narváez appointed captains for each boat. He took charge of one and Cabeza de Vaca another. Estevan climbed into the boat commanded by Dorantes and Castillo.

Almost fifty men crowded into each vessel. The boats were so full the sides were barely above water.

For a month they sailed along the coast, searching in vain for their ships. The sun beat down. Thirst nearly drove them crazy. They passed several rivers. One of them (the Mississippi) was so strong the current pushed them away from shore. Someone put his hand in the water. It was not salty! Estevan and the others gulped it down.

The boats tried to stay together, but they got separated in a storm. Then, in November 1528, a little over a year after they had left Spain, the pounding surf flung forty Spaniards ashore on an island. The place was either Galveston or Matagorda (Texas), but the Spaniards called it Malhado, the place of misfortune.

Fierce Karankawa Indians lived on Malhado. At first, they brought food to the Spaniards, but soon all the men became slaves. They were forced to carry wood on their bruised backs. The Indians scratched them with their fingernails, kicked them, and pulled out their beards.

One day, the Indians ordered the Spaniards to cure people. "We are not doctors," they protested, but the Indians stopped giving them food. The men were desperate. They said some prayers and made the sign of the cross. To their astonishment, the sick Indians got up and said they were well.

For five long years, the Spaniards worked for their Indian masters, but they got separated when they were traded to other tribes. Eventually, only Estevan, Dorantes, Castillo, and Cabeza de Vaca were still alive.

Estevan's life fell into a pattern as the Indians moved from place to place in search of food. In the fall he had gathered pecans on the mainland. In winter he was near the coast where fish and clams were plentiful. In the spring he gathered blackberries.

There was never enough to eat. Everyone was hungry. "Do not worry," said the Indians. "When the tuna comes, your stomachs will be full."

For them, the happiest time of the year was the six months they came together far away from the coast. There they ate prickly pear cactus with the red fruit on it. The Indians squeezed out the juice and drank it. They dried the plant they called tuna and pounded the peel into flour.

One fall, while gathering pecans, the Spaniards were all in the same place. There was a joyful reunion. Soon they were planning an escape. "We will meet during prickly pear season next year," they said. But when the next summer came, the Indians quarreled and left before the men could escape.

Another year went by. When prickly pear season came, they met again. "I am leaving when the moon is full," said Cabeza de Vaca, and the others quickly agreed to join him.

In September 1534, when the moon was full, Estevan and the three Spaniards raced away.

$\mathcal{A}$s the men fled westward, they met another tribe. At first, the Indians ran away, but Estevan ran after them. "Wait!" he said, "Tell us where your houses are."

The Indians knew about the healings, and that night the men were surrounded by crowds of Indians complaining of terrible headaches. Castillo said a prayer, and their pain went away.

The Indians brought gifts of prickly pear and deer meat. It was more than the men could eat, but the Indians would not take it back. All night they sang and danced.

The Spaniards kept moving north and west as long as the rivers flowed toward Malhado. They had no wish to return there.

News of the healings spread. So many sick people came that even Estevan had to act like a doctor.

At one place the Indians would not let them leave. During that winter, they starved while the Indians ate spiders and worms and snakes. When the prickly pears came again, they sneaked away.

At the next place they were hungrier than ever. They made mats and combs to trade for something to eat.

As they moved from tribe to tribe, the Spaniards observed strange customs. One tribe ate mesquite beans mixed with dirt. Another would not allow women to move while the men were drinking a strong tea.

The four men crossed deserts, rivers, and mountains. "Go this way," advised the Indians. If the Spaniards had listened, they would have reached their destination much sooner. But they looked at the rivers and saw that the water still flowed back toward Malhado.

"No," they said, and they headed west into the tall mountains.

Indians went with them on the way. Guides from one tribe led them to the next place.

Everywhere the men went, sick people came to be healed. Mothers brought their babies to be blessed. Estevan happily mingled with all those who came.

The Indians thought the Spaniards were gods and piled up all their belongings as an offering. At one place they presented the men with gourds which had floated down the river. "The gourds have magic powers," said the Indians.

Days turned into months as they walked through places no person from Europe knew existed.

After crossing nearly a thousand miles (Texas), the Spaniards came to a large river (the Rio Grande) and followed it north. Turning west, they entered high mountains (the Rockies). Finally, among the peaks (in New Mexico), the rivers flowed away from Malhado. Only then did they turn south.

Crossing dry, sun-scorched land (Arizona and northern Mexico), they finally entered green valleys sandwiched between mountain ridges (western Mexico). They pushed ahead to reach New Spain, which lay somewhere ahead.

Along the way, the guides began to rob each village they came to. "Do not be sad," the guides told the villagers. "You will get more things when you take these men to the next place."

The Spaniards tried but could not stop the robbery. They refused to keep any of the goods and ate only the food they needed. They gave away everything else.

Still the gifts came. At one place, Dorantes received five arrowheads made of crystals that looked like emeralds. They named another place the Village of Hearts because the Indians gave them six hundred deer hearts as a gift.

One day, some Indians gave them a copper rattle with a face on it. This rattle was more important than anything else they had received. Estevan saw the power that the copper rattle gave the Spaniards.

$\mathcal{W}$eeks went by. They followed the rivers south, hoping to find their countrymen.

One day, they stopped short. An Indian approached. Tied to a cord around his neck was a sword buckle!

"Where did you get that?" they asked.

The Indian replied, "Men with beards like yours came on horses and killed our people with lances."

Slave traders were capturing Indians! Cabeza de Vaca became angry when he heard this, but the news also meant that their countrymen were close by.

Estevan and Cabeza de Vaca set out to find the slave traders. A week later, when they found the kidnappers, the men on horseback could only stare. Eight years had gone by since the Narváez expedition had been heard from!

The slave traders made a false promise to stop kidnapping the Indians and sent the men on a route where they would most likely be killed.

It was not long before they realized what had happened. With the help of Indian guides, they reached Culiacán (Mexico) on April 1, 1536. The mayor, who had heard of their return, led a large crowd in a joyous welcome for the four survivors.

Even though the men had struggled to reach civilization again, they found it hard to adjust to life. They put on heavy, scratchy clothes again, but they found it hard to sleep on a bed. They were more comfortable sleeping on the floor. It took a long time to get used to things they had left so long ago.

23

After the welcome in Culiacán, they continued on to Mexico City, the capital of New Spain. The Spanish had destroyed the Aztec capital of Tenochtitlán and built their new city right on top of it.

Once again they arrived to great fanfare. Everyone was curious to see them. The Viceroy welcomed them in the name of the King of Spain.

Once they got to Mexico City, the four men went different ways. Cabeza de Vaca sailed for Spain but returned to the New World for a short time as governor of South America. Castillo and Dorantes stayed in New Spain. Castillo became rich, and Dorantes married a rich widow and had many children.

But for Estevan it was different. Once back under Spanish rule, he became a slave again.

$\mathcal{E}$veryone listened as the adventurers told tales of their strange adventures and their suffering. They spoke of Indians and their customs. They described deserts, mountains and the minerals they had seen.

They had found no gold, but many believed they had been near the Seven Cities of Cibola. It was said that Cibola had walls built of gold, and everyone wanted to find the place.

The Viceroy first gave Dorantes permission to lead an expedition to find Cibola, but for some reason he didn't go.

Instead, Francisco Coronado took his place, and Estevan was given to the Viceroy so he could act as a guide for Coronado.

In March 1539, Estevan and Father Marcos of Niza left to scout a route to Cibola. Estevan cheerfully set off, retracing the route he had traveled before. In his hand was the copper rattle that gave him power.

Estevan moved along faster than Father Marcos. "Go ahead," said the priest, "but let me know what you find. If the news is good, send me a cross the size of my hand. If it is very good, make the cross larger."

Estevan raced away. As he approached each town, he sent his Indian guides ahead with the rattle as a sign of authority. The Indians in the town then had food and shelter ready when he got there.

When Father Marcos came to the first town, the cross waiting for him was the size of a man!

Father Marcos hurried to catch up, but Estevan didn't wait. At each town, he left larger and larger crosses.

Estevan was far ahead when he reached Hawikuh, a Zuni Indian village that was reported to be the first of the Seven Cities of Gold. The mud walls of the two-story houses may have looked golden in the sun, but they were not made of precious metal.

As usual, Estevan sent the rattle into town, but this time the Zuni chief angrily threw it on the floor. "Do not come into Hawikuh!" he said.

The terrified Indian guides returned with the message, but Estevan was not afraid. "It is sometimes this way," he said. "They will change their minds." He was sure the rattle would protect him, and he went up to the town.

The Zuni Indians seized him and locked him and his guides in a house outside the city. They were given no food or water that whole day. Then, one of the guides escaped, but the Indians killed Estevan when he ran out of the house.

The guide raced back to Father Marcos and told him what had happened. Father Marcos came close enough to see Hawikuh, then he gave everything he had to his Indian guides and returned home with the terrible news. Coronado marched northward anyway.

Estevan, the dark-skinned slave, died at Hawikuh on May 20, 1539. Nobody ever found the cities of gold, but the world learned much about the North American continent because Estevan was one of four men who had walked across it.

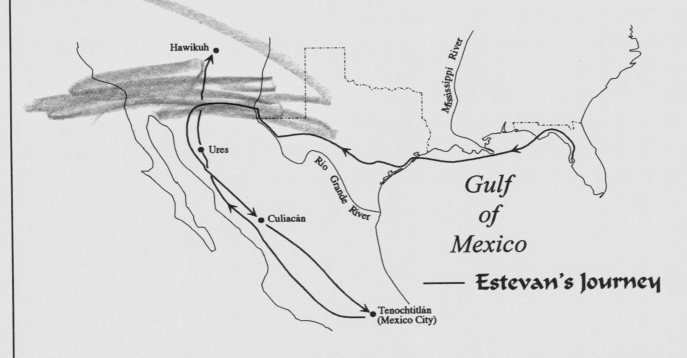

Hawikuh

Ures

Culiacán

Mississippi River

Rio Grande River

Gulf
of
Mexico

——— Estevan's Journey

Tenochtitlán
(Mexico City)

Text set in 14 pt. Swiss Roman type
with chapter initial letters in 40 pt. WaldorfScript
Printed on 90# Mead Endleaf paper
Cover art by Russ Clark
Design by Sanchez Associates
Printing and binding by Walsworth

Zuni fetish based on a representation from Frank H. Cushing's
Second Annual Report of the Bureau of Ethnology,
Washington D.C. 1883.